PUBLIC LIBRAR W9-BPR-422 BIA

Basketball

Basketball

Mike Kennedy

Watts LIBRARY™

Franklin Watts
A Division of Scholastic Inc.
New York • Toronto • London • Auckland • Sydney
Mexico City • New Delhi • Hong Kong
Danbury, Connecticut

Note to readers: Definitions for words in **bold** can be found in the Glossary at the back of this book.

Photographs © 2003: AllSport USA/Getty Images: 32 (Brian Bahr), 50 (Todd Warshaw); AP/Wide World Photos: 37 (Darron Cummings), 40 (Eric Drotter), 2 (Bob Galbraith), 22 (Al Grillo), 6 (Will Kincaid), 35 (Mark Lennihan), 27 (John Lovretta/The Hawk Eye), 20 (Susan Ragan), 19 (Dean Rutz), 49 (Nick Wass), 21 (David Zalubowski), 8, 15, 17, 43; Basketball Hall of Fame: 9, 11 top, 12; California Sports, Inc.: 47; Corbis Images: 5 right, 13, 14, 44, 48 (Bettmann), cover (Duomo); Getty Images: 28 (Stephen Dunn), 29 (Nick Wilson); NCAA Photos: 5 left, 25, 34 (Rich Clarkson), 38 (Brian Gadbery), 30 (Ryan McKee); PhotoEdit/Dennis MacDonald: 51; Smith College: 11 bottom; UCLA Athletic Department: 18.

The photograph opposite the title page shows Hall of Famers Magic Johnson (left) and Isiah Thomas (right), friends and rivals during their NBA careers.

Library of Congress Cataloging-in-Publication Data

Kennedy, Mike (Mike William), 1965–
    Basketball / Mike Kennedy.
       p. cm.—(Watts library)
    Summary: Reviews the history of basketball, how it is played, the rules of the game, and introduces readers to some of basketball's greatest players.
    Includes bibliographical references and index.
    ISBN 0-531-12274-3 (lib. bdg.)   0-531-15591-9 (pbk.)
    1. Basketball—United States—History—Juvenile literature. [1. Basketball.] I. Title. II. Series.
GV885.1 .K47 2003
796.323—dc21

2002015339

© 2003 Scholastic Inc.
All rights reserved. Published simultaneously in Canada.
Printed in the United States of America.
1 2 3 4 5 6 7 8 9 10 R 12 11 10 09 08 07 06 05 04 03

Contents

Basketball has gone from an "overnight sensation" to a sport enjoyed worldwide by players of all ages.

Chapter One

Night Moves

Basketball is played just about everywhere in the world. But it took more than 100 years to become the game fans love today. Still, that's pretty good for a sport that was literally invented overnight! In 1891, Dr. James Naismith was given fourteen days to devise an indoor game that would keep a bored and unruly gym class occupied during the cold winter months in Massachusetts. Having **procrastinated** for thirteen days, Naismith began laying out the basics on the evening of the fourteenth day and finished early the next morning. A few hours later he was explaining the rules of his new game to a group of wide-eyed students at a YMCA in Springfield.

The Good Doctor

For American men and women in the late 19th century, physical fitness and team sports were fast-growing passions. Leading experts preached the benefits of exercise. Baseball was the nation's favorite sport, and millions played and watched it every spring and summer. In the fall, fans turned their attention to football, which was beginning to develop a loyal following. Come winter, they were out of luck. The idea of an indoor team sport wasn't even a consideration.

Dr. Naismith changed all that. A star athlete during his college days in Canada, he analyzed the most popular team sports of the times. He also reflected on games he enjoyed as a kid, including one called "Duck on a Rock." From this patchwork he created basketball.

Naismith's original version was different from today's. Peach baskets were used as goals, there was no backboard,

Dr. James Naismith, born in Canada in 1861, is recognized as the father of basketball.

Name Game

Naismith's students initially wanted to call their new sport Naismith-Ball. He rejected the idea, and everyone soon agreed on Basket-Ball.

Some of basketball's first players pose for a team photo in 1891.

and a soccer ball served as the official ball. Nine players a side took the floor. No one thought of dribbling, so passing was the only way to advance the ball. Fouls were called for **infractions** of all kinds, not just bumping an opponent or slapping him on the wrist or arm.

Though shooting the ball into the basket was extremely difficult, basketball was still a hit. In the spring of 1892, an article on the sport appeared in a newsletter sent to the more than two hundred YMCAs nationwide. Thousands of men soon tried their hand at this new game. Women began to play, too.

Zoning In

As basketball's popularity rose, so did the skill level. The rules became more **sophisticated**. Early on, games were rough and scores were low. Some people referred to basketball as indoor football. In fact, made baskets were called field goals, which is still true today. To open up the sport, the number of players was gradually decreased to five per side. Baskets were increased in value from one point to two points. Rules prohibiting dribbling were relaxed, too.

Improvements in equipment followed. The first basketball, complete with laces like those on a football, was introduced in 1894. Backboards came into widespread use a year or two later. Players switched from leather shoes to rubber-soled shoes. By 1913, nets hung from every gymnasium rim.

By the turn of the century, colleges everywhere had basketball teams. Schools in various regions of the country banded together in **intercollegiate** leagues. Squads began squaring off against opponents in other states.

Caged In

In basketball's early days, spectators were part of the action. When the ball went out of bounds, the team that retrieved it was awarded possession. This often led to wild scuffles in the stands that left fans bruised and bloodied. Starting in 1896, cages made from chicken wire were erected around indoor basketball courts to keep the ball from bouncing into the bleachers. Cages remained in use until the 1930s, and basketball players are still referred to as "cagers" from time to time.

At the University of Chicago, John Schommer and Pat Page teamed up for the college game's first **formidable** one-two punch. At the University of Wisconsin, coach Walter "Doc" Meanwell pioneered new, fast-paced strategies on offense. In fact, the zone defenses played today were created in part to slow down the powerful Badgers.

Meanwhile, the pro game was taking root in New York, New Jersey, and Pennsylvania. By the late 1890s, teams regularly paid top players to appear in exhibition games. The Amateur Athletic

The first basketballs had laces, which sometimes caused shots to fly in weird directions.

Students at Smith College take the floor in basketball's early days. Women have been playing the sport for as long as men.

Renaissance Men

Except in the South, **segregation** in basketball was not a major issue. That was partly because of an all-black professional team called the New York Renaissance.

Founded by Bob Douglas in 1922, the Rens made their home in Harlem in New York City, the capital of African-American culture during the Roaring Twenties. Douglas schooled his team in imaginative offense, tough defense, and unparalleled sportsmanship. The Rens jammed the stands with admiring fans every time they took the court. Pictured above is Charles T. Cooper, one of the team's many stars.

Union staged the first international basketball tournament at the 1901 Pan-American Exposition in Buffalo, and a squad of professionals known as the Buffalo Germans won the title. Other pro teams soon embarked on regional tours, including the Troy Trojans and their center Eddie Wachter.

A Helping Hand

During the 1920s professional leagues sprouted in the Midwest and Northeast. The New York Celtics were the class of the sport, thanks to Nat Holman and Joe Lapchick. They packed **armories** and arenas with enthusiastic fans wherever they played.

Pro basketball players, however, were decades away from earning the huge salaries they make today. The top stars often took jobs with large corporations that sponsored basketball squads of their own. The prospect of a steady paycheck, especially when times got tough in the 1930s, was too tempting to pass up.

On college campuses, meanwhile, coaches began to realize that whatever

As demonstrated in this photo of Bill Bradley, a college and NBA star of the 1960s and 1970s, the influence of Hank Luisetti's running one-handed shot was felt for decades.

their teams lacked in talent, they could make up for in strategy and training. This trend made Dr. Naismith **bristle**. Now in charge of the University of Kansas program, he believed that excessive coaching would ruin the game. But his successor with the Jayhawks, Forrest "Phog" Allen, proved him wrong. Allen devised an innovative defensive strategy that switched from zone to man-to-man. His coaching system inspired other coaches such as Ward "Piggy" Lambert, Doc Carlson, and Clair Bee.

By the late 1930s, youngsters with dreams of playing for collegiate powerhouses began experimenting with new moves. A teenager from California named Hank Luisetti revolution-ized the sport with a running one-handed shot. Until he came

Rain or Shine

Long before America began assembling its first star-studded Dream Team for the 1992 Olympics, basketball was lucky just to be considered an Olympic sport. After a pair of demonstration tournaments in the 1920s, basketball made its official debut at the 1936 Summer Games in Germany.

Unfortunately, organizers staged the competition outdoors on grass. Heavy rains during the final between the United States and Canada turned the game into a mudfest! After the Americans won 19–8, Olympic officials chose to move all future tournaments inside.

along, everyone used two hands to launch the ball toward the basket and kept both feet planted firmly on the ground.

When Luisetti joined Stanford, the balance of power in college basketball began to shift. For years, schools in New York City ruled the sport. Now teams from the West and Midwest rose to challenge them. This rivalry helped lay the

St. John's, a college in New York, won the NIT four times from 1943 to 1965.

groundwork for the National Invitation Tournament (NIT) held in Madison Square Garden. In 1939, with the support of coaches from other regions of the country, the National Collegiate Athletic Association (NCAA) started a rival post-season tournament. Today the winner of the NCAA Tournament is crowned college basketball's national champion.

Clock Work

While World War II sapped most sports of their best and brightest, basketball was spared because the U.S. military hesitated to recruit exceptionally tall men. George Mikan, who stood nearly seven feet tall, was among those not drafted. In turn, he spearheaded the era of the "big man," a trend that sent shockwaves throughout basketball. College coaches who didn't have a tall center had to find ways to beat teams that did. This led to the development of the **fast break**, as smaller players such as Bob Cousy countered immense size with speed.

In the 1950s, coach Adolph Rupp combined the best of both worlds at Kentucky. The Wildcats annually featured a roster of big, versatile players. They won the NCAA Tournament four times in eleven

Bob Cousy, nicknamed the "Houdini of the Hardwood," helped usher in the fast break with the Boston Celtics in the 1950s.

years and contributed to the dramatic rise in college basketball's popularity. But a series of gambling **scandals**, including one at Kentucky, threatened the game's **credibility**.

As the college game stumbled, the pros picked up steam. Starting in 1937, the National Basketball League (NBL) established itself as the first professional organization with staying power. Over the next decade, the league cultivated an increasingly exciting brand of basketball, signing college stars such as Buddy Jeannette and bringing big-time sports to the small Midwest cities of Akron, Oshkosh, and Sheboygan. Then in 1947, the Basketball Association of America (BAA) opened for business. While the BAA couldn't match the NBL's talent, it operated in major cities, including New York, Boston, and Philadelphia. In July 1949, the leagues merged and were renamed the National Basketball Association (NBA).

The NBA grew in talent and prestige as college superstars such as Dolph Schayes, Vern Mikkelsen, and Ed Macauley joined the league. But pro games all too often **degenerated** into ugly foul-fests or boring stalling contests. Entering the 1954–1955 season, the NBA adopted a twenty-four-second shot clock to make contests more exciting. This rule required teams to shoot within twenty-four seconds of gaining possession of the ball. Squads were forced to hurry up the court and score quickly. The twenty-four-second clock also gave an edge to players who could go one-on-one and create their own shots.

Taking Off

Basketball moved above the rim in the 1950s—and fans loved it. Bill Russell of the Celtics led the way. A wiry 6-foot-10 (208 centimeters) center, he relied on amazing quickness and leaping ability to dominate on defense. He could also start and finish Boston's devastating fast break. From 1957 to 1969, the Celtics won eleven championships.

The Celtics' **unprecedented** run drew new fans to the NBA. So did the exposure the league received from TV contracts with NBC and ABC. Every Sunday viewers were treated to a game featuring players like Jerry West, Elgin Baylor, Sam Jones, and Jerry Lucas. The most memorable contests matched Russell against Wilt Chamberlain, the greatest offensive force in basketball history.

In 1967, a group of businessmen started a league called the American Basketball Association (ABA). They filled their rosters with cast-offs from the NBA, and signed young hotshots such as Rick Barry and Mel Daniels. With new rules like the three-point basket (a long shot from the outside worth

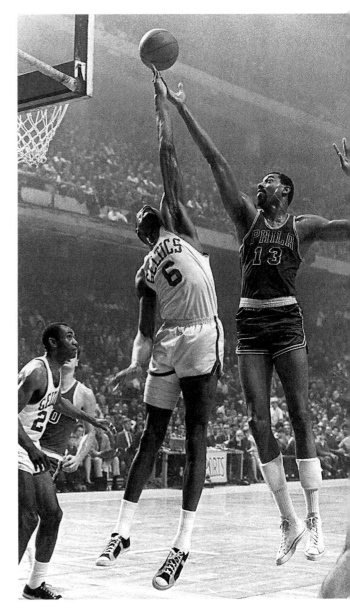

Bill Russell and Wilt Chamberlain battle above the rim for a rebound.

Lew Alcindor (before he changed his name to Kareem Abdul-Jabbar) rises high to release his famous skyhook for UCLA.

three points), the ABA offered a high-flying, high-scoring brand of basketball that the NBA couldn't match. In effect, the league was thumbing its nose at its stuffy rival (the ABA played with a red, white, and blue ball!).

In 1976, the NBA agreed to absorb four ABA teams and welcome all of the league's remaining stars on existing rosters. But professional basketball soon fell on hard times. Drug scandals and failing attendance pushed the NBA toward bankruptcy.

Luckily, college basketball was healthy and popular. In the 1960s coach John Wooden built a dynasty at UCLA that saw his Bruins win the national championship nine times in eleven years. This drew more attention to the college game, and made national stars of All-Americans such as Lew Alcindor (who later changed his name to Kareem Abdul-Jabbar), Elvin Hayes, and Pete Maravich.

College basketball continued to flourish in the 1970s and 1980s. The "Final Four" of the NCAA Tournament attracted bigger and bigger television audiences. It also focused atten-

Bobby Knight (right) relied on strict discipline and precise execution from his players to become one of college basketball's greatest coaches ever.

tion on brilliant coaches such as Dean Smith and Bobby Knight, and later John Thompson and Mike Krzyzewski.

Two players who rose to **prominence** in college also fueled the NBA's resurgence. When Larry Bird and Earvin "Magic" Johnson joined the league, the pro game received the boost it needed. They were followed by Michael Jordan, who electrified fans with his acrobatics and intense desire to win. Many experts consider him the greatest player of all time.

Today stars like Kobe Bryant and Kevin Garnett have taken the torch from Jordan, propelling one of many new trends in

Women at Work

The women's game got its start at Smith College in the 1890s and has grown steadily. During the 20th century, the sport made important **inroads** at the high school and college levels. It took its biggest steps in the 1970s when legislation was passed guaranteeing female athletes the same opportunities as their male counterparts. Today the NCAA women's tournament is televised nationwide, just like the men's. But the most significant moment in women's hoops came at the 1996 Olympics in Atlanta, Georgia, when the U.S. team stormed to the gold medal. Their awesome performance helped launch the Women's National Basketball Association, the most successful women's professional league to date. Sheryl Swoopes (#7 for Team USA in 1996) was one of the WNBA's first stars.

basketball. By bypassing college and jumping directly to the NBA from high school, both have shown how swiftly the next generation of players is evolving. The same is true internationally. The United States no longer dominates the way it

Kobe Bryant (#8) is leading the NBA's newest wave of stars into the 21st century.

used to at the Olympics, and foreign players are taking up more and more spots on NBA rosters. Meanwhile, women's basketball gains in popularity every year, both in college and the pros. What do these developments say about the future of basketball? That even though the sport has already reached levels once thought unattainable, the game has the potential to soar even higher.

Shooting is only one part of basketball. Passing and defense are important skills, too.

Chapter Two

Taking the Floor

Lots of kids think that shooting is the only talent required to succeed on the basketball court. Nothing could be further from the truth. Basketball is a game of teamwork that demands a variety of skills.

Flexible Five

Five players take the floor for a basketball team. The point guard and off guard make up the **backcourt**. The small forward, power forward, and center comprise

Court Report

A regulation NBA or college court is 94 feet (28.5 m) long and 50 feet (15 m) wide, with a basket at each end. In some older gyms where recreational leagues are played, the court is smaller. The division line separates the floor in half. The circle at midcourt is where players gather for the **jump ball** at the start of each game.

Out of bounds is determined by the endlines and sidelines, which stretch all the way around the court. If a player with the ball steps on one of these lines or outside them, action is halted and the ball is awarded to the opposing team. The same thing happens when the ball touches these lines or lands outside them.

the **frontcourt**. In basketball lingo, each position is often referred to by a designated number: point guard, 1; off guard, 2; small forward, 3; power forward, 4, and center, 5.

Of course teams often stray from this traditional lineup. For example, coaches who don't have a big center sometimes use three guards. Coaches lucky enough to have more than one center may choose to play two at the same time.

Playing in the backcourt requires quick hands and feet, a reliable outside shot, poise under pressure, and the ability to see the entire floor. The point guard is the leader on offense. His primary job is to set up his teammates for good shots. The

Sharp Shooter

Long before the designated hitter came along in baseball, there was a position in college basketball known as the designated free-throw shooter. As the name suggests, one player on the floor was chosen by his coach to attempt all of his team's foul shots—no matter who got hacked. The rule remained in effect until 1923.

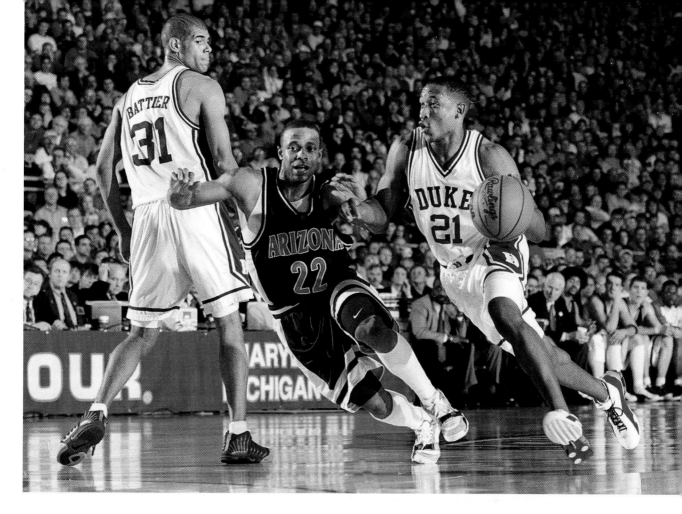

off guard is viewed as more of a scorer, whether attempting jump shots from the outside or slashing to the hoop for a layup. On defense, both guards try to disrupt the opponent's offensive flow.

Size and strength are the first two attributes that come to mind when discussing frontcourt players. Quickness, sure hands, and a soft shooting touch are important, too. The center usually sets up in the low "post," the area on the floor around the basket. This is the best place to make use of his height on offense and defense.

Duke guard Chris Duhon tries to dribble around Jason Gardner of Arizona during a college game.

Post-Up Note

Why is the area around the basket called the post? When basketball was invented, most gyms of the era had large support beams that extended from the floor to the ceiling. These posts happened to stand on each end of the court where the baskets were suspended just above the foul line. While the posts were eventually moved to accommodate the playing of basketball, coaches and players continued to refer to this spot as the post.

The power forward is often expected to do the dirty work on the floor. That means setting **picks** to free teammates for open shots on offense, bumping and jostling with opponents in the lane on defense, and rebounding the ball on both ends. The small forward is often the most dangerous offensive player on the floor. For example, when his team grabs a defensive rebound, he looks for an opportunity to race down the court and convert a layup on the fast break.

Substitutions are also a vital part of basketball. Running up and down the floor can be very tiring. Coaches rarely play their five starters an entire game without a rest. That's why the players on the bench must always stay alert and prepared. They are asked to enter the game on a moment's notice, and join the action ready to go at full speed.

Dribbling and Passing

What's the key to handling the ball effectively? Dribble as low to the ground as possible. This makes it hard for a defender to bat the ball away. Also, keep your attention focused on what's

happening in front of you, and be ready to pass to open teammates.

To avoid having the ball stolen, practice dribbling low to the ground.

Passing requires sound technique as well. Practice throwing crisp passes with two hands. Cradle the ball in your fingers near your chest, and then push it out. The chest pass never touches the floor, while the bounce pass **ricochets** up off the hardwood. Smart players don't **telegraph** their passes. In

Dash and Dish

The ability to dribble by a defender and toward the rim is known as penetration. This strategy forces a second defender to help out, leaving a teammate on offense open. The player with the ball can either speed all the way to the hoop for a layup, or pass to someone else for an easy shot at the basket.

In the Zone

In addition to man-to-man, coaches employ zone defenses. In these schemes, each player is assigned a certain area of the floor, and guards anyone who roams into this space.

In man-to-man defense, each player on the floor is assigned to guard an opponent one-on-one.

other words, they make a defender believe they're going to pass in one direction, then fire the ball in another.

There's plenty to do when you don't have the ball. Move around, and try to find soft spots in the defense. This is the best way to get free for good shots at the basket.

Defense and Rebounding

Defending a player man-to-man is a test of technique and concentration. Start with your feet shoulder-width apart and your knees slightly bent. Stay on your toes, and be ready to shuffle to the left or right. Try to keep your body between your opponent and the basket at all times. Don't worry about blocking shots. It's more important to prevent the opposition from getting into easy scoring position.

Good defenders learn as much as they can about the strengths and weaknesses of their opponents. They also know when to help out a teammate. For example, if your center gets mismatched against a guard,

28

you may have to leave your assigned player and offer assistance.

When a shot is missed, it's anyone's ball. But there's more to rebounding than jumping high for the ball. The proper way to establish rebounding position is called **boxing out**. To do this, use your legs and rear end to nudge your opponent away from the hoop. When the ball bounces off the rim, leap forward to snatch it.

On a rebound of a missed shot, the ball is up for grabs.

Good shooters keep their eyes on the rim, not the ball, when releasing a shot.

Right and Left

Whether you're right-handed or left-handed, learn to shoot and dribble with both hands. It's much more difficult to defend a player when you don't know which way he's going.

Shooting

Everyone wants to be a good shooter. Is there a trick to putting the ball in the basket? Not really. Good shooters have plenty of natural ability, but they also practice constantly.

Focus on the rim when shooting. To release a shot with a soft touch, keep the ball in your fingers, rather than in the palm of your hands. Don't shoot only with your arms and hands. Try to transfer the energy in your feet and legs all the way up to your finger tips.

Bend the wrist of your shooting hand toward the basket when releasing the ball. This technique, known as following through, puts backspin on the shot. This motion increases the chances of the ball going in if it hits the rim.

Remember that shooting is only one phase of the game. Ballhandling, passing, rebounding, and defense are just as important. Players only concerned with scoring usually aren't very good teammates.

Height Advantage

Some tall players develop a bad habit of dribbling before shooting when they receive a pass near the basket. If you have a height advantage, hold the ball high where defenders can't knock it away.

Good refs follow the action up and down the court, and are always in position to call a foul.

Chapter Three

Blowing the Whistle

In basketball, with each made shot and every turnover, the teams on the court switch between offense and defense. The game's hectic pace is a physical challenge for everyone. Players slap at the ball, bump into each other, and even tumble to the floor sometimes. That's why referees are needed. They keep an eye on the action at all times. When a ref spots a foul or violation, he blows his whistle, and play stops immediately.

Game Time

Pro games are divided into four 12-minute quarters, with half-time coming after the second quarter. The rules are somewhat different in college, where contests are split into two 20-minute halves. High schools usually play four 8-minute quarters.

Baskets are worth two points, unless attempted beyond the three-point line. In the NBA this line extends 22 feet (6.5 m) from the hoop along the wings, and arches out to a maximum distance of 23 feet, 9 inches (7 m, 23 cm). The three-point arc is closer to the basket in all other levels of play.

Countdown

The team on offense has 10 seconds (only 8 seconds in the NBA!) to advance the ball across the midcourt line. If it fails to do so, the opposition gains possession.

Shots attempted beyond the three-point line are worth one point more than those taken inside the arc.

Jump Start

Until 1937, teams returned to mid-court for a jump ball after every made basket. A squad with a tall center could dominate a game by winning every tip. Fortunately that's not the case today. In the NBA, aside from the start of a game, a jump ball is held any time two opposing players **simultaneously** control the ball. In college, however, teams simply alternate possession when the ball is tied up.

Excessive contact is likely to draw either an offensive or defensive foul.

When a player is awarded free throws, he shoots from the foul line, which is 15 feet (4.5 m) from the basket. The charity stripe also serves as the top of the foul lane, the rectangular area around the basket at each end of the court. Players on offense without the ball are not allowed to stand in the lane for more than three seconds. On foul shots, rebounders cannot enter the foul lane until the ball touches the rim.

Foul Mood

Even the best defenders commit fouls. What is illegal? Knocking into an opponent while trying to block a shot, grab a rebound, or steal the ball is almost always whistled. Refs, however, use their discretion. Some

Shooter's Edge?

Arithmetic shows that making a basket shouldn't be as difficult as it seems. Though the rim is 10 feet (3 m) above the court, it measures 18 inches (46 cm) in **diameter**. By contrast, the diameter of a standard basketball is a little less than 9 inches (23 cm). (Women in the pros and college use a slightly smaller ball.) In other words, two balls can fit inside the rim at the same time!

officials let players get away with lots of contact, while others call a game to the letter of the law.

Defensive fouls committed against a player attempting a shot result in free throws. Two free throws are awarded for a two-point shot and three for a three-point shot. One bonus free throw is awarded if the player who is fouled makes the shot while being hacked.

Other fouls, such as banging into an opponent when going for a rebound, are known as non-shooting. They become shooting fouls, however, if a team commits too many. A player who fouls too many times is kicked out of the game, or fouled out.

No Interference

On defense, players can't block a shot as it drops down toward the rim. This is known as goaltending, and the shooter is awarded a basket. There is offensive goaltending, too. If a player on offense taps in a ball judged to be inside an imaginary cylinder that extends above the rim, the basket is waved off.

Getting Offensive

Refs can also call fouls on the team that has the ball. The most common foul is charging. This occurs when the player shooting or dribbling runs into an opponent who has established position on defense. Other offensive fouls include elbowing a defender or shoving him when trying to get free for a shot. When an offensive foul is called, the defensive team is awarded the ball. Sometimes an offensive foul results in free throws.

Players on offense can also be whistled for violations, which carry less severe consequences than fouls. The three-second rule described earlier is an example. So is traveling, which is moving with the ball without dribbling it. The team on offense loses possession of the ball when a violation is called.

In this photo, the offensive player (in white) is guilty of charging after he barrels into the defender.

The dunk has become basketball's most exciting play.

Chapter Four

Above the Rim

For more than five decades, basketball was an **earthbound** game, with most players relying on quickness, deception, and elaborate plays just to get an open shot. In many cases, small players had an advantage over tall ones. That changed forever with the introduction of the shot clock in the 1950s. Almost overnight, the focus shifted to tall, athletic players who could soar high above the hardwood.

Jump Start

Kenny Sailors, who led Wyoming to the 1943 NCAA championship, and NBA Hall of Famer Paul Arizin were among the first to master the jump shot.

A Basketball Renaissance

No one knows for sure when basketball took to the air. In the mid-1930s at the tryouts for the first U.S. men's Olympic basketball team, fans at Madison Square Garden in New York City watched in awe as the McPherson Globe Oilers dunked the ball during pre-game warm-ups. According to historians, however, the New York Renaissance was already exploring a vertical style of hoops.

The all-black Rens featured wonderful athletes such as Clarence "Fat" Jenkins and Bill Yancey, both of whom competed professionally in other sports. They raced up and down the court, threw behind-the-back passes, and scored baskets in all sorts of imaginative ways. Their brand of basketball caused many fans and players to look at the sport in a new way.

By the 1940s, basketball's pace of play had picked up considerably, and one-handed shooting was all the rage. Players also began to realize that jumping before they shot and releasing the

Today's players still use many of "razzle-dazzle" skills pioneered in the 1920s by the New York Rens.

40

ball at the **apex** of their leap was an effective way to score over a stationary defender.

Tall Tales

The greatest leaper of the 1950s and 1960s was Bill Russell. But what made him different was that he used his amazing ability as a defender and rebounder. It was not unusual for Russell to block a dozen shots and haul down 30 rebounds in a game, both in college and the pros.

Russell's exploits gave smaller players a lot to think about. Learning to rise off the hardwood and control their bodies in midair was now crucial to competing against athletic big men. Elgin Baylor was the first to show the way. An explosive 6-foot-5 (165 cm) forward, he developed an amazing arsenal of offensive moves that made him a superstar.

Wilt Chamberlain also was influenced by Russell. The silky smooth 7-footer (213 cm) combined great defense and eye-popping offense. He once scored 100 points in a game, and averaged just above 50 for an entire NBA season. His

If You Can't Beat Him

What did college coaches do when they found they couldn't stop Chamberlain? They changed the rules. They widened the lane and **outlawed** offensive goaltending, which prevented "Wilt the Stilt" from stuffing home errant shots on their way toward the rim. The NCAA also prohibited players from taking off from the foul line and dunking their free throws. Chamberlain, a world-class high jumper, favored this technique in high school.

duels with Russell in the 1960s were the greatest spectacle in basketball.

Fans quickly gained appreciation for basketball above the rim. They thrilled to the breathtaking combination of grace and power displayed by NBA stars such as Oscar Robertson and Gus Johnson. In college, UCLA's Lew Alcindor followed in Russell's and Chamberlain's footsteps. In fact, the NCAA ruled the dunk illegal during Alcindor's college career and waited five years to **reinstate** it.

Jam Session

Perhaps the best showcase for basketball's high-flying stars was the ABA. During the 1960s and 1970s, the league encouraged its players to be as creative as possible. Julius "Dr. J" Erving, Connie "The Hawk" Hawkins, and David "Skywalker" Thompson were tops among a dynamic group of dunkers.

In 1976, Erving focused even greater attention on the jam when he won the ABA's first slam dunk contest. Eight years later the event became the centerpiece of the NBA's All-Star

Slam Sisters

Dunking has never been a prominent part of the women's game—mainly because few have been able to jam. In 1984, Georgeann Wells became the first to dunk in a college game. The next to do it was Charlotte Smith ten years later. Takeisha Lewis was the first high schooler to throw one down. In recent years more women have shown the right stuff. The most spectacular has been Michelle Snow, who can slam it home with one hand.

weekend. In the years that followed, players of all shapes and sizes took the crown, including 5-foot-8 (172 cm) Spud Webb and Dominique Wilkins, known as the "Human Highlight Film."

Of course, many fans believe that no one will ever match the artistry of Michael Jordan. During his prime, he was able to hang in the air and glide past defenders with amazing ease and beauty. Who today has the potential to be like Mike? Some say Kobe Bryant. Others say Vince Carter. It's really anyone's guess. In fact, you might say the answer is up in the air.

Julius Erving, known as Dr. J, astounded fans with his amazing leaping ability and body control.

Larry Bird led the Boston Celtics to three NBA titles from 1981 to 1987.

Chapter Five

Hardwood Heroes

Although basketball's best all-time players took different paths to greatness, all share something in common. They knew that, on their own, they could set individual records. But they believed in the team concept, and understood that working together with their teammates was the only way to win.

Early Risers

The game's first big star was Nat Holman. Known as "Mr. Basketball," he

A Pair of Bobs

Bob Davies and Bobby McDermott are often overlooked by historians, but each had a major impact on the game. Davies, a magician with the ball, was the first to use the behind-the-back dribble for more than just show. McDermott was the last of the great set shooters. Once he was across half-court, any shot was in his range.

played on the Original Celtics, and helped bring legitimacy to the world of the pros. During the 1920s his Celtics took on all comers up and down the East Coast. The team rarely lost, thanks to Holman's pinpoint passing from the pivot and innovative defensive strategies, including the man-to-man switch.

In the mid-1930s Angelo "Hank" Luisetti made headlines at Stanford. Graceful and handsome, Luisetti looked like an All-American and played even better. It wasn't long before young players nationwide were copying his one-handed style.

As more and more kids experimented with basketball, **enterprising** coaches began working with towering teenagers who were once thought to be too uncoordinated to star on the hardwood. At 6 feet, 10 inches (208 cm) tall, George Mikan was the first center to dominate at both ends of the court. "Big George" led the Minneapolis Lakers to four titles in the NBA's first five years.

Going Big—And Small

Bob Cousy defined the role of the modern point guard. Lightning quick and fabulously flashy, the "Houdini of the Hardwood" forced a change in basketball philosophy, as defenders had to move in tighter in man-to-man defense. Traditionalists frowned on Cousy's style of play—until they realized it could deliver championships. He won six NBA titles with the Boston Celtics in the 1950s and 1960s.

The other essential piece of Boston's dynasty was Bill Russell. "Number Six" revolutionized basketball with his tenacious rebounding and awesome shot blocking. In all he collected a record thirteen titles in college and the pros.

At 7–1 (216 cm), with the quickness of a guard, Wilt Chamberlain was the greatest scorer in NBA history.

Russell's arch rival was the incomparable Wilt Chamberlain, whose Hall-of-Fame career spanned fourteen seasons. "The Big Dipper" was fast and powerful, and could literally score at will. It wasn't until Chamberlain became a true team player, however, that he won an NBA championship.

Getting Creative

The **advent** of the NBA's twenty-four-second shot clock put a premium on pure scorers. Suddenly, players who could create their own shots—with a head-and-shoulders fake, a quick dribble, or by using their bodies to make space on the floor—became offensive weapons. Among those who rose to stardom during this era were Elgin Baylor, Tom Heinsohn, Bob Pettit, Tom Gola, and Bailey Howell.

The Whole Package·

By the 1960s, the best players prided themselves on their all-around skills. Jerry West, who owned perhaps the sweetest jump shot in basketball history, was also a suffocating defender. Named to the NBA's All-Defensive team four times, he became famous during his fourteen-year career for blocking shots—even though he was a 6-foot-3 (191 cm) guard.

Oscar Robertson played bigger than his 6-foot-5 (196 cm) frame, too. The "Big O" approached basketball with a football player's mentality. Rough and rugged, Robertson was fearless around the basket. During the 1961–1962 season he averaged a **triple-double** with 30.8 points per game, 12.5 rebounds, and 11.4 assists.

Walt Frazier was another guard who could do it all. Nick-named Clyde for his stylish persona off the court, he was a

Jerry West of the Lakers tries to shoot over Bill Russell of the Celtics during a game between Los Angeles and Boston.

deft ballhandler, sharp passer, and accurate shooter. Frazier, who guided the New York Knicks to two NBA titles, perfected the art of the steal.

Winning Attitudes

Point guard Earvin "Magic" Johnson took the concept of versatility to a new level. At 6 feet, 9 inches (206 cm), he could see the floor in ways that shorter players couldn't, and provided tremendous match-up problems for opposing teams. In an emergency, Magic played any position, including center. His Lakers won five championships with him at the helm.

One of the few players who could match Magic's feel for the game was Larry Bird. A **throwback** to basketball's early days, he couldn't jump high or run fast, but his instincts were uncanny. A forward with the Celtics, Bird always seemed to be in the right place at the right time, and was lethal with the game on the line. He was voted NBA MVP three straight years, and led Boston to three titles.

49

Sky's the Limit

No center ever had a more polished offensive game than Kareem Abdul-Jabbar. His skyhook was probably the most effective shot ever. At 7 feet, 2 inches (219 cm) , Abdul-Jabbar could launch the ball over any defender with amazing accuracy. His 38,387 points are the most in NBA history.

Well past his 30th birthday, Michael Jordan could still blow by defenders nearly half his age.

Women of Distinction

Though women have played the game as long as men, the first female star didn't come along until after World War II. Her name was Nera White, and she ruled women's hoops for fifteen years. By the 1970s, the women's game featured a dazzling array of talented players, including Carol Blazejowski, Nancy Lieberman, Lucy Harris, and Ann Meyers. A decade later Lynette Woodard, Anne Donovan, Cheryl Miller, and Teresa Edwards followed in their footsteps.

The birth of the WNBA in 1996 gave women an exciting new stage to strut their stuff. Cynthia Cooper, who led the Houston Comets to four titles, has received the most acclaim, but players such as Lisa Leslie, Sheryl Swoopes, and Chamique Holdsclaw (above, during her days at the University of Tennessee) aren't too far behind. Each deserves recognition as a pioneer. Their influence has helped women's basketball continue to evolve and improve. Now a new set of stars— from Sue Bird, the 2002 women's collegiate player of the year, to Australia's Lauren Jackson, the latest international sensation to hit the WNBA—is ready to become part of this legacy.

No discussion of basketball's greatest players is complete without Michael "Air" Jordan. Most people believe he is the best ever. Jordan captured six championships and five MVPs with the Chicago Bulls, and a national title at North Carolina. At the heart of his success was an intense desire to win and the ability to make those around him better.

Of today's players, Kobe Bryant and Shaquille O'Neal have already claimed multiple NBA crowns, and appear motivated to go for more. Waiting in the wings is an assortment of young, hungry players. Jason "Jay" Williams was the nation's best player at Duke in 2002, but will his skills translate into an NBA title? Youngsters such as Kevin Garnett and Tracy McGrady are perennial All-Stars. A teenager from Ohio named LeBron James may have the brightest future of all.

Whoever steps up and becomes the game's next super-star, one thing is certain: They will understand that basketball is—and always will be—a team sport. Even if you're not the next Michael or Cynth', the game still has plenty to offer. Most important, it will teach you the value of teamwork. And through teamwork, just about anything is possible, on the hardwood and off it.

Some players dream of a career in the NBA or WNBA. Others just want to have fun.

Timeline

1891	Dr. James Naismith invents basketball.
1894	The first ball made just for basketball is introduced.
1895	The value of a basket is increased to two points.
1901	The Buffalo Germans win the AAU championship at the Pan-American Exposition.
1913	The modern drop-through net is introduced.
1917	Sporting goods company Converse debuts its All-Star basketball sneaker.
1919	Forrest "Phog" Allen takes over for Naismith as the coach of Kansas.
1923	The New York Renaissance team is founded by Bob Douglas.
1928	Charging fouls are called for the first time.
1931	The AAU organizes a women's basketball tournament in Los Angeles, California.
1934	Hank Luisetti joins Stanford and revolutionizes basketball with his running one-handed shot.
1936	Basketball makes its official debut at the Olympics.
1938	Temple wins the first National Invitation Tournament.
1939	The University of Oregon wins the first NCAA Tournament.
1946	Transparent backboards are introduced to give fans behind the basket a better view of the action.
1949	The Associated Press publishes its first college basketball poll.
1954	The NBA introduces the twenty-four-second shot clock.

1957	Bill Russell leads the Boston Celtics to their first of eleven NBA titles in thirteen years.
1962	Wilt Chamberlain scores 100 points in a game against the New York Knicks.
1966	Texas Western becomes the first team with an all-black starting five to win the NCAA championship.
1967	The ABA makes its debut.
1972	The Association for Intercollegiate Athletics for Women begins sponsoring a national championship tournament.
1973	UCLA wins its seventh NCAA title in a row.
1976	The NBA and ABA merge.
1979	Larry Bird and Magic Johnson meet in the NCCA Final, then both go on to the NBA.
1984	The U.S. women's basketball team wins its first goal medal at the Olympics.
1986	College basketball adopts the three-point shot.
1992	The USA's first "Dream Team" appears at the Olympics, and captures the gold medal with ease.
1996	The WNBA debuts after the U.S. women take the gold at the Olympics.
1998	Tubby Smith, Kentucky's first African-American coach, guides the Wildcats to the national title.
2000	Kobe Bryant, who jumped to the pros directly from high school, teams up with Shaquille O'Neal to lead the Los Angeles Lakers to the NBA title.
2003	After having come out of retirement in 2001, Michael Jordan retires again.

Glossary

advent—the arrival of something important

apex—top

armory—a building where military equipment is made or stored

backcourt—a basketball term that refers to a pairing of guards on the same team

box out—a basketball term for establishing position before grabbing a rebound

bristle—to react angrily

credibility—to inspire trust

deft—moving in a quick and skillful way

degenerate—to develop into a worse condition

diameter—the distance from one point on a circle straight through the center to another point

earthbound—influenced by the laws of gravity which attract things toward the earth's surface

enterprising—showing a willingness to try new ideas

fast break—a basketball term used to describe an offensive strategy in which a team grabs a defensive rebound then races toward the other hoop for a layup

formidable—difficult to deal with or overcome

frontcourt—a basketball term that refers to the players who make up the front line of forwards

infraction—failure to follow a rule or law

inroad—a gradual progession towards something

intercollegiate—involving more than one college or university

jump ball—A way to determine possession of the ball. The referee tosses the ball up between two players and both try to tap it to a teammate.

outlaw—to prohibit

pick—a term used in basketball to describe when a player uses his body to block a defender and create an open shot for a teammate

procrastinate—to delay, avoid

prominence—the condition of being distinguished or well-known

reinstate—to bring something back into use

ricochet—to hit a surface and bounce away in a different direction

scandal—a situation that cause public outrage

segregation—keeping ethnic, racial, religious, or gender groups separate

simultaneous—done, happening, or existing at the same time

sophisticated—complex, advanced, and up-to-date

telegraph—to make it obvious that you're about to do something

throwback—something with characteristics from any earlier era

triple-double—a statistical term in basketball that describes when a player hits double figures in three different categories

unprecedented—having no equivalent to come before

To Find Out More

Books

Anderson, Dave. *The Story of Basketball*. New York, NY: William Morrow and Company, Inc., 1997.

Rutledge, Rachel. *The Best of the Best in Basketball*, Brookfield, CT: The Millbrook Press, 1998.

Stewart, Mark. *Basketball: A History of Hoops*. Danbury, CT: Franklin Watts, 1998.

Stewart, Mark. *The Final Four*. Danbury, CT: Franklin Watts, 2002.

Stewart, Mark. *The NBA Finals*. Danbury, CT: Franklin Watts, 2003.

Any of the basketball biographies in the New Wave series by Mark Stewart published by the Millbrook Press.

Organizations and Online Sites

http://www.alleyoop.com
Up-to-the-minute news and stats from the NBA and NCAA.

http://www.usabasketball.com
Official site of USA Basketball. Keep tabs on the national teams that represent the United States in international competition, including player profiles and statistics.

Naismith Memorial Basketball Hall of Fame
http://www.hoophall.com/
Official site of the Naismith Memorial Hall of Fame. Learn about all of the hall's members, which include foreign players and women, through detailed biographies and statistics.

National Basketball Association
http://www.nba.com
Official site of the National Basketball Association. Read about your favorite players, and follow links to your favorite teams.

NCAA Basketball

http://www.ncaabasketball.net

Official site of NCAA basketball. Learn about all of the hall's members through detailed biographies and statistics.

Women's Basketball Hall of Fame

http://www.wbhof.com

Official site of the Women's Basketball Hall of Fame. Find out about the greatest women players in basketball history.

A Note on Sources

In researching this book, I tried to reference as many sources as possible. I consulted another author named Mark Stewart, who has written books on basketball, including biographies of famous players. I also went to my local library and checked out a wide variety of books. Web sites on the Internet, including the one hosted by the National Basketball Association, were helpful as well.

—*Mike Kennedy*

Index

Numbers in *italics* indicate illustrations.

About the Author

From Ichiro to the Indy 500 and the Super Bowl to skateboarding, Mike Kennedy has covered it all in the world of sports. A graduate of Franklin & Marshall College, he has profiled athletes such as Sammy Sosa, Tony Hawk, and Venus and Serena Williams. Mike has contributed his expertise to other books by Grolier/Scholastic, including *The World Series*, *The Super Bowl*, and *The NBA Finals*. He is also a co-creator of JockBio.com (*www.jock-bio.com*), a unique website that profiles popular sports personalities.

His other titles in this series are *Baseball*, *Football*, *Ice Hockey*, *Roller Hockey*, *Skateboarding*, and *Soccer*.

MAR 8 2004